Japan Explained: Japanese Culture through Authentic Texts

日本文化の魅力と多様性

Akiko Tsuda
Kayoko Kinshi
Chris Valvona

EIHŌSHA

ACKNOWLEDGMENT

The editor and publisher acknowledge permission to reproduce
15 copyright articles in this book:
Used by permission of Hiragana Times Incorporated.
In addition, Keiko Ono, the author of the articles
in Chapter 9 and 11,
kindly gave us permission to reprint them.

PRINTED IN JAPAN

はじめに

　ひらがなタイムズは、1986 年の創刊で、100 ヶ国以上の人に読まれている外国人の会話に役立つ情報や内容を解説する日英バイリンガルマガジンです。本書 Japan Explained: Japanese Culture through Authentic Texts「日本文化の魅力と多様性」は、同紙の中から、選りすぐりの話題を取り上げ、日本事情を学びながら、英語の技能を向上させることを目標とした教材です。必ずしも、ユニットの順にしたがって進めなければならないわけではありません。各ユニットの構成は次のようになっています。

Warm-up Question

　このユニットで学ぶトピックについて考える問題です。
＊日本語でも、英語でも構わないので考えてみましょう。

Check Your Vocabulary

　このユニットで学ぶ語彙について、定義や綴りを学びます。

Note-taking

　音声を聴いて、聞こえたフレーズを書き取ってみましょう。

Dictation

　二回目以降のリスニングでは、細部を聞き取って、空欄を埋めます。答え合わせをしたら、音読やシャドーイングをすると良いでしょう。

Speed Reading

　1 分間でどのくらいの速さで読めるか、測り、記録しておきましょう。

Comprehension Check

　本文の理解度を確認するための問題です。ペアやグループで確認してもよいでしょう。

Extension Activities

　重要語彙や表現を学んでみましょう。

Write or Speak about Yourself

　このユニットを振り返り、英語で自己表現してみましょう。

　最後に、本書の構想から出版に至るまで、佐々木元氏、下村幸一氏をはじめとして、英宝社の皆様には大変お世話になりました。心より感謝の意を表します。

著者一同

Contents

Chapter 1

嘘レビュー

Fake Reviews

....

▶ Warm-up Question

....

Have you ever left a review for something you bought online?

Do you read online reviews before you purchase anything on the internet or via an app? Do you trust those reviews?

....

▶ Check Your Vocabulary

....

左側の単語にもっとも近い意味をもつ表現を右から選びましょう。

1. thriving (adj.)　（　）　　a. good or useful
2. positive (adj.)　（　）　　b. very successful
3. bot (n.)　（　）　　c. a formal statement saying that something is true
4. competitor (n.)　（　）　　d. a computer program that works automatically
5. testimony (n.)　（　）　　e. a person, team, or company that is trying to be more successful than others

Note-taking 🔊 **2**　本文を聴きながらノートを取りましょう。（英語でも日本語でも構いません）

2

1   Stores, such as department stores and convenience stores, which used to be the main commercial outlets in Japan, are now decreasing in numbers. On the other hand, online shops are increasingly thriving. Nowadays it is said that customers' comments about the

5   products on sale play an important role in buyers'$_{50}$ decision-making processes. However, it was recently reported on TV and in other media outlets that most of these reviews are fake. It was revealed that there are many people writing reviews for products they have not purchased, working part-time for websites that give rewards in

10   exchange for positive reviews. Among $_{100}$ these was the case of a company in a certain foreign country that was writing and posting them in great volumes using bots. The following are characteristics of fake reviews: numerous five-star evaluations, many posts appearing on the same day for a product, and product descriptions

15   that are vague. When $_{150}$ the Japanese expressions are somewhat unnatural, it can be an indication that they have been created overseas, and when there are many one-star reviews, that they were ordered by competitors. Some years ago, the news that some stores were hiring people to create "sakura" (fake queues) caused quite a

20   stir. $_{200}$ It is said that the reasons for this kind of practice lie in the Japanese tendency to trust the testimony of others. (223 words)

▶ Dictation

音声を聴いて空欄を埋めなさい。一回目はスロースピード、二回目はナチュラルスピードで録音されています。答え合わせをしたら、音読しましょう。（　　/6点）

The (1　　　　　　　) are characteristics of fake reviews: (2　　　　　　　) five-star evaluations, many posts appearing on the (3　　　　　　) day for a (4　　　　　　), and (5　　　　　) descriptions that are (6　　　　　　).

☐ **1st Speed Reading**

wpm

▶ Comprehension Check

本文を読んで、以下の問いに答えなさい。

1. What used to be the main commercial outlets in Japan?

2. What are some websites giving people in exchange for positive reviews?

3. Having many one-star reviews indicates they were probably ordered by whom?

☐ **2nd Speed Reading**

wpm

▶ Extension Activities

犯罪関係の重要単語

選択肢から選んでみましょう。

日本語	英語
殺人	
泥棒	
すり	
万引き	
放火	
贈収賄	
密輸	
誘拐	

pickpocket   smuggling   homicide   shoplifting kidnapping   arson   bribery   theft

▶ Write or Speak about Yourself

以下の質問について，答えてみましょう。

Q： Describe a time you were very happy or very disappointed with something that you ordered online.

A：

Chapter ❷

和の思考

The Concept of Harmony

》Warm-up Question

Do you often argue with other people? Who do you argue with, and what do you argue about?

》Check Your Vocabulary

左側の単語にもっとも近い意味をもつ表現を右から選びましょう。

1. enact (v.)　　　(　)　　a. to live in a place
2. dogmatism (n.)　(　)　　b. to make a proposal into a law
3. dispute (n.)　　(　)　　c. relating to farming and farmers
4. inhabit (v.)　　(　)　　d. an argument or disagreement
5. agrarian (adj.)　(　)　　e. stating your opinions in a strong way and not accepting anyone else's opinions

Note-taking 🔊❹ 本文を聴きながらノートを取りましょう。（英語でも日本語でも構いません）

In every age, conflicts between individuals and nations occur all over the world. In Japan, however, a spirit of cooperation has been fostered since ancient times. In the 7th century, Prince Shotoku created "The Seventeen Article Constitution." This was the first law to be enacted in Japan. Unlike the modern $_{50}$ constitution, it taught morals and proper ways of thinking to the nobles and bureaucrats involved in politics. It begins with the first article: "Cherish harmony above all else, and do not fight unnecessarily." It is characterized by its warning against dogmatism and repeated advocacy of the importance of discussion. This $_{100}$ spirit is also found in the Constitution of Japan, which is said to have been created at the initiative of the U.S. It states: "The Japanese people seek international peace and will never use force as a means of settling international disputes." In addition, most people who visit Japan, $_{150}$ both now and in the past, have commented on how safe and peaceful the country is. It can be assumed that "the concept of harmony" developed from the idea of avoiding conflicts by being considerate of and sympathetic to others in a cultural climate of an island nation inhabited by $_{200}$ agrarian people, whose ethnicity was almost completely homogeneous. The Japanese language has developed in a way that reflects the Japanese way of thinking. You could say that "the concept of harmony" is the very essence of "Nihongo Spirit."

(237 words)

▶ Dictation

音声を聴いて空欄を埋めなさい。一回目はスロースピード、二回目はナチュラルスピードで録音されています。答え合わせをしたら、音読しましょう。(/6点)

In every (1   ), conflicts between (2   ) and (3   )
occur all over the (4   ). In Japan, however, a spirit of (5   ) has
been fostered since (6   ) times.

☐ **1st Speed Reading**

wpm

▶ Comprehension Check

文章をよく読み、正しい (T)、間違い (F)、この文章からは読み取れない (?)のいずれか、あてはまるものを記入しなさい。

1. The Seventeen Article Constitution was Japan's first law. (   )

2. The modern constitution of Japan contains a similar spirit to the Seventeen Article Constitution. (   )

3. Japan's weather helped to develop the "concept of harmony." (   )

☐ **2nd Speed Reading**

wpm

▶ Extension Activities

人の様子に関する重要英単語

選択肢から選んでみましょう。

日本語	英語
激怒して	
快適で	
不機嫌で	
楽観的で	
悲観的で	
寛大で	
単調で	
陽気で	

grumpy	pessimistic	monotonous	furious
hilarious	generous	comfortable	optimistic

▶ Write or Speak about Yourself

以下の質問について，答えてみましょう。

Q： **What do you do to avoid conflict?**

A：

Chapter 3

子ども食堂

Children's Cafeterias

▶ Warm-up Question

Have you ever volunteered? What did you do?
Why do you think people volunteer?

▶ Check Your Vocabulary

左側の単語にもっとも近い意味をもつ表現を右から選びましょう。

1. disparity (n.)　　(　) 　　a. to obtain something that is difficult to get

2. household (n.)　　(　)　　b. a family or group of people who live together in a house

3. procure (v.)　　(　)　　c. to have just enough money to buy the things you need

4. initiative (n.)　　(　)　　d. difference, usually relating to the money people earn or their status

5. make ends meet (　)　　e. a plan or activity that is done to solve a problem or
   (idiom.)　　　　　　improve a situation

Note-taking 🔊 ⑥ 本文を聴きながらノートを取りましょう。(英語でも日本語でも構いません)

1 "Children's Cafeterias" are places where meals are served mainly by volunteers from the local community, and began in earnest around 2015, exceeding 6,000 locations by the end of 2021. Children's Cafeterias are communities that provide free or low-price meals to

5 children and their parents who are unable to eat adequately, 50 due to financial difficulties or other circumstances. Currently, economic disparity is widening in Japan, with one in seven children living in poverty. The nationwide expansion of Children's Cafeterias is said to be due in part to social issues imparted by an increase of low-income

10 and single-parent households. In the beginning, 100 some families were hesitant to use the service because they did not want their poverty and family situation to be exposed to the public. In spite of that, families making use of the service have continued to increase, now becoming a place where parents of poor families, who tend 150 to

15 be disconnected from society, may communicate with one another. Management organizations are challenged to make ends meet with operating costs, when considering cafeteria space, volunteer staff, and procuring foodstuffs. It is a difficult situation to sustain. Taken as a matter of course, such projects should be carried out by 200 the

20 government. Although some local governments have taken on their own initiatives, their participation has not been adequate. In the past, there was a culture in Japan where neighbors helped each other on a daily basis. The Children's Cafeteria reminds us of the poor days when there was no government support. (250 words)

▶ Dictation

音声を聴いて空欄を埋めなさい。一回目はスロースピード、二回目はナチュラルスピード
で録音されています。答え合わせをしたら、音読しましょう。（　　/6点)

Children's Cafeterias are (1　　　　　　　) that provide (2　　　　　　　) or low-price
meals to children and their (3　　　　　　　) who are unable to eat (4　　　　　　　),
due to (5　　　　　　) difficulties or other (6　　　　　　).

□ **1st Speed Reading**

wpm

▶ Comprehension Check

以下の質問に答えなさい。

1. Who mainly serves the meals at Children's Cafeterias?

2. What is currently getting wider in Japan?

3. According to the article, who should be responsible for carrying out projects such as Children's Cafeterias?

□ **2nd Speed Reading**

wpm

▶ Extension Activities

重要な社会問題の表現

選択肢から選んでみましょう。

日本語	英語
高齢化社会	
身分制度	
栄養失調の子どもたち	
社会参加	
人権	
人種差別	
特権階級	
情報格差	

malnourished children	privileged class	information gap	class system
racial discrimination	human rights	social participation	aging society

▶ Write or Speak about Yourself

以下の質問について，答えてみましょう。

Q： **Would you consider doing volunteer work in the future?**
Why or why not?

A：

Chapter 4

日本人の「建前」

Japanese "Public Face"

▶ Warm-up Question

Do you ever hide your true feelings when you are communicating with someone? Why?

▶ Check Your Vocabulary

左側の単語にもっとも近い意味をもつ表現を右から選びましょう。

1. constitution (n.) ( ) a. allowed by law
2. interpret (v.) ( ) b. to use something for your advantage
3. legitimate (adj.) ( ) c. to accept or allow something although you do not like it
4. tolerate (v.) ( ) d. to explain the meaning of something
5. exploit (v.) ( ) e. a set of laws and principles that a country's government must obey

Note-taking 🔊 **8** 本文を聴きながらノートを取りましょう。（英語でも日本語でも構いません）

1　In Japan there is a phrase that goes: "*honne to tatemae*." This means "one's true feelings and outward opinions." This represents the difference between one's emotions and one's public stance. This is said to be an aspect of the Japanese mindset. For instance, as a
5　reflection of World War II, 50 the Japanese constitution states that Japan has no military. However, as this could be interpreted to mean that it is legal to maintain a force to defend the country from invasion, a legitimate standing army exists under the label of a self-defense force. In Japan, while gambling is illegal with 100 the
10　exception of things like authorized horse and bicycle races, there are pachinko parlors everywhere – a game which is often called "Japanese-style pinball." You can exchange balls won in a pachinko game for prizes displayed in the parlor. The prizes can be exchanged for cash at a prize exchange 150 booth located close to the parlor under
15　the pretext that you are selling them. While thus publicly staying true to the letter of the law, the Japanese have a tendency to tolerate certain practices that exploit loopholes. For this reason non-Japanese people sometimes criticize the Japanese for saying one thing and 200 doing another. However, if you look at this from another angle,
20　"*honne to tatemae*" is a way of resolving issues without making waves and could be thought of as a kind of wisdom particular to the Japanese. Some people believe that more flexibility in our interpretation of the rules could 250 play an important role in resolving international conflicts.　(258 words)

▶ Dictation

音声を聴いて空欄を埋めなさい。一回目はスロースピード、二回目はナチュラルスピードで録音されています。答え合わせをしたら、音読しましょう。（　　/6点）

This represents the (1 　　　　　　) between one's (2 　　　　　　) and one's
(3 　　　　　) (4 　　　　　　). This is said to be an (5 　　　　　　) of the
Japanese (6 　　　　).

☐ **1st Speed Reading**

wpm

▶ Comprehension Check

文章をよく読み、正しい（ **T** ）、間違い（ **F** ）、この文章からは読み取れない（ **?** ）のいずれか、あてはまるものを記入しなさい。

1. The Japanese mindset of "*honne to tatemae*" dates back hundreds of years. （　　）

2. In Japan, it is never legal to gamble on bicycle races. （　　）

3. Foreigners sometimes complain that Japanese people's words and actions are not the same. （　　）

☐ **2nd Speed Reading**

wpm

▶ Extension Activities

重要な句動詞（**Phrasal Verbs**）

選択肢から選んでみましょう。

日本語	英語
見せびらかす	
脱ぐ、離陸する	
熟考する	
捨てる	
試着する	
振り向く	
用心する	
書き留める	

write down	show off	watch out	take off
think over	turn around	throw away	try on

▶ Write or Speak about Yourself

以下の質問について，答えてみましょう。

Q： **Describe a time when you hid your true feelings.**

A：

Chapter 5

判官びいき

Sympathy for the Underdog

▶ Warm-up Question

When a stronger sports team plays a weaker team, which team do you support? Why?

▶ Check Your Vocabulary

左側の単語にもっとも近い意味をもつ表現を右から選びましょう。

1. regime（n.） （ ） a. giving a warning
2. clan（n.） （ ） b. a particular government or system
3. vie（v.） （ ） c. to force someone to have the same ideas as you
4. cautionary（adj.）（ ） d. to compete very hard with someone to get something
5. impose（v.） （ ） e. a large group of families who often share the same name

ⓝote-taking 🔊 ⑩ 本文を聴きながらノートを取りましょう。（英語でも日本語でも構いません）

 **10**

¹ *Hangan-biiki* is a word that expresses sympathy or support for a person in a weak position. Hangan refers to the official title given to Minamoto no Yoshitsune by the court. He was the younger brother of Minamoto no Yoritomo, who was the first shogun of the

⁵ Kamakura Shogunate (12th century) ₅₀, which was the first samurai regime. Yoshitsune was the warrior who destroyed the Heike clan, which had been vying for power with the Genji clan, and was most instrumental in paving the way for the establishment of the Kamakura shogunate regime. At that time, political power was

¹⁰ concentrated with the ₁₀₀ emperor at the imperial court in Kyoto, but Yoritomo, who was supported by the warriors of Kanto, strengthened his control of his own domain. Yoritomo became angry with Yoshitsune for accepting the position at the Imperial Court in Kyoto without his permission, and destroyed him before he could bring

¹⁵ disorder ₁₅₀ among the ranks of the samurai under his control. People sympathized with Yoshitsune's tragic end. Later, many stories were written about him. In kabuki, movies and novels, he has been cast as a tragic hero. Siding with the underdog or *hangan-biiki* is said to be a sentiment that is unique ₂₀₀ to the Japanese and is often seen to this

²⁰ day at sports events and in TV dramas. However, it is sometimes used as a cautionary tale about not having the sense to understand the bigger picture. On the other hand, other people say that the interpretation of this story is ₂₅₀ up to the individual and that you shouldn't impose your viewpoint on others. (263 words)

▶ Dictation

音声を聴いて空欄を埋めなさい。一回目はスロースピード、二回目はナチュラルスピードで録音されています。答え合わせをしたら、音読しましょう。（　　/6点）

Yoritomo became angry with Yoshitsune for (1　　　　　　　　) the position at the Imperial Court in Kyoto without his (2　　　　　　　), and (3　　　　　　　) him before he could bring disorder among the ranks of the samurai under his (4　　　　　　　). People (5　　　　　　　) with Yoshitsune's (6　　　　　　　) end.

☐ **1st Speed Reading**

wpm

▶ Comprehension Check

以下の文章について、義経（**Yoshitsune**）についての文章か、頼朝（**Yoritomo**）についての文章か、書きなさい。

1. He had the title of Hangan.　（　　　　　　　）

2. He was the older brother.　（　　　　　　　）

3. He had support from the Kanto warriors.　（　　　　　　　）

4. He accepted a position at the Imperial Court in Kyoto.　（　　　　　　　）

5. Many stories were written about him after he died.　（　　　　　　　）

☐ **2nd Speed Reading**

wpm

▶ Extension Activities

身分に関する重要単語

選択肢から選んでみましょう。

日本語	英語
天皇	
皇太子	
王族	
主君	
商人	
農夫	
百万長者	

the Crown Prince   millionaire   emperor
peasant   merchant   lord   royalty

▶ Write or Speak about Yourself

以下の質問について，答えてみましょう。

Q： **Describe a time when you were the underdog.**

A：

Chapter 6

不都合な真実

An Inconvenient Truth

▶ Warm-up Question

What examples of climate change can you think of?

▶ Check Your Vocabulary

左側の単語にもっとも近い意味をもつ表現を右から選びましょう。

1. horror（n.）　　（　）　a. able to be trusted or believed
2. withdrawal（n.）　（　）　b. something that is very terrible or shocking
3. advocate（v.）　　（　）　c. to become less strong or extreme
4. credible（adj.）　（　）　d. to express support for a particular idea
5. subside（v.）　　（　）　e. the act of no longer taking part in an activity

N ote-taking 🔊 **12** 本文を聴きながらノートを取りましょう。（英語でも日本語でも構いません）

1   This year, record temperatures around the world were more than 40 degrees Celsius, sparking the breakout of many wildfires. In Japan, record-breaking hot days continued from June. Furthermore, torrential rains caused flooding while rivers and lakes dried up. In

5   2006, the American movie "An Inconvenient Truth," pointing out the horrors 50 of abnormal weather caused by global warming, was screened to sound an alarm to the world. Prior to that, in 1997, the Kyoto Protocol was enacted to establish an international framework for combating the threat of climate change. In 2016, the United

10 States and China, the largest greenhouse gas emitters 100, agreed to the protocol. But then Trump, a global warming skeptic, became the president of the United States and announced the withdrawal from the agreement. Global warming was an inconvenient topic for the Trump administration, which advocates for a resurgence of

15 manufacturing. Due to this, it was reported that he 150 had a number of pseudoscientists tell the public that global warming was not credible. Regardless of its credibility, President-elect Biden announced his intention to return to the agreement shortly after taking office. Amidst issues of global warming, Russia's invasion of

20 Ukraine occurred in February of this year. In Japan, due 200 to energy shortages, the re-use of nuclear power plants is about to begin, despite the risks involved. With neither global warming nor the threat of viruses subsiding, the people, who seek to cling to immediate gains, and the politicians, who seek to exploit the public

²⁵ mind under the mask of ₂₅₀ justice, continue to have a history that is as sterile as ever. （263words）

🔊 ⑬

▶ Dictation

音声を聴いて空欄を埋めなさい。一回目はスロースピード、二回目はナチュラルスピードで録音されています。答え合わせをしたら、音読しましょう。（　　/6点）

In (1　　　　　　), the (2　　　　　　) movie "An Inconvenient Truth," (3　　　　　) out the horrors of abnormal (4　　　　　　　) caused by global warming, was (5　　　　　) to sound an (6　　　　　) to the world.

☐ **1st Speed Reading**

wpm

▶ Comprehension Check

文章をよく読み、正しい（ **T** ）、間違い（ **F** ）、この文章からは読み取れない（ **?** ）のいずれか、あてはまるものを記入しなさい。

1. The United States and China agreed to the Kyoto Protocol 19 years after it had been enacted. （　　）

2. President Trump believes that global warming is a serious issue. （　　）

3. When he was President-elect, Biden did not plan to rejoin the Kyoto Protocol. （　　）

☐ **2nd Speed Reading**

wpm

▶ Extension Activities

重要な句動詞（**Phrasal Verbs**）

選択肢から選んでみましょう。

日本語	英語
立ち寄る	
外食する	
屈服する	
じっくり調べる	
電話を切る	
追い出す	
見下す	
指摘する	

look down on   eat out   hang up   drop by
kick out   give in   go through   kick out

▶ Write or Speak about Yourself

以下の質問について，答えてみましょう。

Q： **Describe an example of climate change or extreme weather where you live.**

A：

進化する日本語

The Evolving Japanese Language

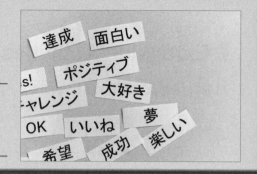

達成　面白い
s!　ポジティブ
大好き
ャレンジ
OK　いいね　夢
希望　成功　楽しい

▶ Warm-up Question

Do you know any Japanese words that were originally from a foreign language? e.g. テレビ

Do you know what language they came from?

▶ Check Your Vocabulary

左側の単語にもっとも近い意味をもつ表現を右から選びましょう。

1. evolve (v.)	( )	a. to cause something
2. modify (v.)	( )	b. to accept or start using something new
3. adopt (v.)	( )	c. to be the same or very similar
4. correspond (v.)	( )	d. to change something, usually in a small way
5. give rise to (phr. v.)	( )	e. to develop gradually over a long period of time

Ⓝote-taking 🔊⑭ 本文を聴きながらノートを取りましょう。（英語でも日本語でも構いません）

1 Convenience stores were introduced to Japan from the U.S. around
   1970. Since there were no stores in Japan with this concept, the
   name "convenience store" was adopted as-is into the Japanese
   language. However, because of its word length, the abbreviation
5 "*konbini*" became widespread. The same goes for the widespread $_{50}$
   use of the word "*terebi*" derived from the word "television."
   Whenever a new cultural concept is introduced from overseas, the
   Japanese take the original language and use it as it is, evolving it into
   the Japanese language. The same was true in ancient times, as the
10 reading parts $_{100}$ of kanji characters introduced from China were used
   as Japanese characters. However, because of the complexity of kanji,
   Japanese created hiragana and katakana by using a part of the kanji
   character. Additionally, Japanese characters replicated sounds similar
   to the original sounds of foreign words such as Chinese and $_{150}$
15 English. That is to say, these foreign words were modified for
   Japanese pronunciation. In other words, it is a Japanization of a
   foreign language. There are 45 sounds in Japanese, all of which can
   be pronounced with their variants, in addition to the long sound and
   double consonants $_{200}$ that are unique to the Japanese language. In the
20 Meiji period (19-20th century), when many concepts that did not
   exist in Japanese were introduced from the West, the Japanese
   created new kanji corresponding to these concepts. For example,
   "democracy" gave rise to the word "*minshu*" meaning people-
   oriented. Such idioms $_{250}$ were reimported by China and are still in
25 use today. The Japanese language is always evolving. (263 words)

▶ Dictation

音声を聴いて空欄を埋めなさい。一回目はスロースピード、二回目はナチュラルスピードで録音されています。答え合わせをしたら、音読しましょう。(　　/6点)

1. Convenience stores were （1　　　　　　　） to Japan from the U.S. around （2　　　　）.
2. However, because of the （3　　　　　） of kanji, Japanese created hiragana and katakana by using a part of the kanji （4　　　　　）.
3. In （5　　　　　） words, it is a Japanization of a （6　　　　　） language.

☐ 1st Speed Reading

wpm

▶ Comprehension Check

文章をよく読み、正しい（ T ）、間違い（ F ）、この文章からは読み取れない（ ? ）のいずれか、あてはまるものを記入しなさい。

1. Convenience stores originated in Japan. （　　）

2. The pronunciation of foreign words is kept the same when used in Japanese. （　　）

3. Japanese has some sounds that are not found in any other language. （　　）

4. The modern Chinese kanji for "democracy" was borrowed from Japanese . （　　）

☐ 2nd Speed Reading

wpm

▶ Extension Activities

日本のことわざ

ことわざになるように、空欄に当てはまる語を選択肢から選んでみましょう。

日本語	英語
あばたもえくぼ	Love is （　　　　　　　　　）.
去る者は日々に疎し	Out of sight, out of　（　　　　　　　　　）.
後悔先に立たず	Don't cry over （　　　　　　　　）.
蛙の子は蛙	Like father, like （　　　　　　　　）.
転ばぬ先の杖	Look before you　（　　　　　　　　）.
触らぬ神に祟りなし	Let sleeping dogs （　　　　　　　　）.

mind	lie	son	milk	leap	blind

▶ Write or Speak about Yourself

以下の質問について，答えてみましょう。

Q： **Describe a Japanese word or concept (e.g. *nemawashi*) that you think should be adopted by other languages.**

A：

Chapter **8**

アニメの魅力

The Attraction of Anime

▶ Warm-up Question

Do you watch a lot of anime?
Why do you think Japanese anime is so popular in Japan and overseas?

▶ Check Your Vocabulary

左側の単語にもっとも近い意味をもつ表現を右から選びましょう。

1. integral（adj.）　（　　）　a. to begin an important activity
2. enthusiasm（n.）　（　　）　b. necessary and important as part of something
3. capitalize（v.）　（　　）　c. a movie, TV show etc. that is based on another work
4. adaptation（n.）　（　　）　d. to take advantage of a situation
5. launch（v.）　　　（　　）　e. a strong feeling of interest and enjoyment about
　　　　　　　　　　　　　　　　something

Note-taking 🔊 **16** 本文を聴きながらノートを取りましょう。（英語でも日本語でも構いません）

¹ Known for being an integral part of Japanese culture, the global popularity of anime is reaching ever greater heights. This summer, 81,000 fans gathered for three days at "Ani-melo Summer Live." Held in Saitama Prefecture, this is one of the world's largest *anison*

⁵ (anime song) music festivals. In addition to ₅₀ this, 26,000 people gathered for two days to watch popular voice actors sing at the "ORE!! SUMMER" open-air festival held in Yamanashi Prefecture. It is said that the appeal of seeing anime songs performed live lies in the electric atmosphere generated by the enthusiasm of both

¹⁰ performers and audience. When ₁₀₀ a voice actor or actress becomes popular they are not only invited to appear at events, but can also release CDs, become radio personalities, or have their image featured in magazines. Voice acting, which was once considered to be a behind-the-scenes job, is now a glamorous occupation for

¹⁵ young people. ₁₅₀ On the other hand, the tourism industry is capitalizing on the popularity of anime. "2.5 Dimensional Musicals," that is adaptations of 2D anime or manga into theatrical plays, have already become a big draw with foreign tourists. The Japan Anime Tourism Association has launched "Japan's Anime Tourism 88 for

²⁰ Anime ₂₀₀ Fans (2018 Edition)." Besides the smash hit "Kimi No Na Wa" ("Your Name"), anime locations such as "Girls und Panzer," "Lucky Star," "Ultraman" and "Evangelion" were selected. Fans of novels or movies used to visit famous locations featured in their favorite works, but nowadays it's anime fans that flock to ₂₅₀ such

²⁵ spots. The fans' enthusiasm for these works seems to be unaffected by the passage of time. （267 words）

▶ Dictation

音声を聴いて空欄を埋めなさい。一回目はスロースピード、二回目はナチュラルスピードで録音されています。答え合わせをしたら、音読しましょう。（　　/6点）

> When a voice actor or actress becomes （1 　　　　　） they are not only invited to
> （2 　　　　　） at events, but can also （3 　　　　　） CDs, become radio
> （4 　　　　　）, or have their （5 　　　　　） featured in （6 　　　　　）.

☐ **1st Speed Reading**

wpm

▶ Comprehension Check

本文を読んで、以下の問いに答えなさい。

1. How many people attended the live event in Saitama?

2. Voice acting is now a glamorous occupation, but how did it use to be thought of?

3. These days, what do anime fans flock to?

☐ **2nd Speed Reading**

wpm

▶ Extension Activities

職業に関する重要単語

選択肢から選んでみましょう。

日本語	英語
技術者	
建築家	
作曲家	
批評家	
編集者	
教授	
顧問	
弁護士	

lawyer   professor   critic   architect
engineer   composer   editor   advisor

▶ Write or Speak about Yourself

以下の質問について，答えてみましょう。

Q： **Describe your favorite anime.**

A：

Chapter 9

名刺交換

Exchanging Business Cards

....

▶ Warm-up Question

....

What do you think are important points to remember when giving or receiving a business card in Japan?

....

▶ Check Your Vocabulary

....

左側の単語にもっとも近い意味をもつ表現を右から選びましょう。

1. crumpled (adj.)　　　（　）　a. to hide or cover something
2. conceal (v.)　　　　（　）　b. to buy something
3. purchase (v.)　　　（　）　c. in a lower position than something
4. beneath (prep.)　　（　）　d. to think that someone is less important than you
5. look down on (phr. v.)（　）　e. crushed into a smaller, bent shape

N ote-taking 🔊 **18**　本文を聴きながらノートを取りましょう。（英語でも日本語でも構いません）

1   In Japan it is customary to exchange cards when meeting someone for the first time in a professional context. It is rude to hand out crumpled cards, since it gives the impression that you are looking down on the person. And, it is also rude to put cards you've received

5   ₅₀ directly into your pocket. When presenting your card, hold it out with both hands so that they can easily read the characters, taking care not to conceal the letters. When holding it out, clearly state your name and the name of your company, "How do you do? I'm Brown of ₁₀₀ ABC company. *Yoroshiku onegai itashimasu.*" It's a good idea

10   to add phrases such as those that follow: "Thank you for giving me your time today," or "I appreciate you taking time out of your busy schedule." Those who have a favor to ask or a product they wish to sell ₁₅₀ should present their business card first, while those who are being asked a favor of or who might be purchasing a product go

15   after. If you are dealing with several people, you should take turns handing over your cards, starting with the person in the highest position. In any case, ₂₀₀ you should be prepared by placing clean business cards in a business card case, and put this somewhere that is easily accessible. When the person you're addressing is already

20   holding out their card, present your card beneath theirs. When you have forgotten to bring your business cards, or you have ₂₅₀ handed them out to so many people that no cards remain, you should apologize as follows: "I'm sorry. My business cards have run out. Please excuse my rudeness." (277 words)

▶ Dictation

音声を聴いて空欄を埋めなさい。一回目はスロースピード、二回目はナチュラルスピードで録音されています。答え合わせをしたら、音読しましょう。（　　/5点)

In any (1 　　　　　　), you should be prepared by placing (2 　　　　　) business cards in a business card (3 　　　　　), and put this (4 　　　　　) that is easily (5 　　　　　).

☐ **1st Speed Reading**

wpm

▶ Comprehension Check

本文を読み、以下の問いに答えなさい。

1. What kind of business cards give a rude impression, like you think you are more important than the other person?

2. If you want to ask a favor, should you give your card first or second?

3. Where should you keep your business cards?

☐ **2nd Speed Reading**

wpm

▶ Extension Activities

ビジネスの重要単語

選択肢から選んでみましょう。

日本語	英語
年金	
社会保険	
配偶者	
扶養家族	
株主	
前任者	
引き抜き	

predecessor   spouse   pension   headhunting dependent   predecessor   shareholder

▶ Write or Speak about Yourself

以下の質問について，答えてみましょう。

Q： **Describe a time you have given or received a business card.**

A：

Chapter 10

空気の読めないお客

Reading between the Lines

▶ Warm-up Question

Are you good at "reading the room"?

* read the room は、「空気を読む」の意。

▶ Check Your Vocabulary

左側の単語にもっとも近い意味をもつ表現を右から選びましょう。

1. feign (v.) 　（ 　） 　a. lack of interest or concern
2. indifference (n.) （ 　） 　b. to pretend to have a particular feeling
3. blankly (adv.) 　（ 　） 　c. to do something in order to make someone less angry
4. mutter (v.) 　（ 　） 　d. in a way that shows no understanding, interest, or emotion
5. pacify (v.) 　（ 　） 　e. to speak quietly, often when complaining about something

▶ Note-taking 🔊 20 本文を聴きながらノートを取りましょう。（英語でも日本語でも構いません）

1 In Japan a culture of "reading the situation" exists. This refers to interpersonal communication; deciding how to act based on the particulars of place and circumstance. The other day I entered a coffee shop with a member of my staff and an American client.

5 Unfortunately there was no space available $_{50}$ for three people to sit together. When I looked around a young man using a smartphone was in a booth that sat four. Next to him was an empty booth that sat two, so if he moved there, we would be able to speak comfortably. The young man looked noticed $_{100}$ us, but feigned indifference. Angry

10 that the young man couldn't read the situation, I said to the waitress "Could you ask him to switch seats?" Then she said, "I can't say such things," and left to fetch an extra seat. Irritated at the young man and the waitress for not $_{150}$ picking up on my signals, I said to him, "Excuse me. Would you mind moving over to the next seat?"

15 He looked at me blankly and did not move. I muttered, "This young man lacks consideration for others," but my staff pacified me, saying in a quiet voice, "Now now, $_{200}$ please calm down." We ended up sitting down at the booth that sat two with extra seating attached. It seemed that the American client did not understand why I was

20 irritated. Sometime after we began talking, the smartphone of the young man next to us rang. Then he began to $_{250}$ have an enjoyable conversation in a language I had never heard. I realized that though the young man had appeared to be Japanese, he was a foreigner. And, realizing that I had misread the situation, I became even more

25 irritated. (278 words)

▶ Dictation

音声を聴いて空欄を埋めなさい。一回目はスロースピード、二回目はナチュラルスピード
で録音されています。答え合わせをしたら、音読しましょう。(/6点)

1. The other day I (1   ) a coffee shop with a member of my staff and an American (2   ).
2. (3   ) there was no space (4   ) for three people to sit together.
3. When I looked around a young man using a smartphone was in a (5   ) that (6   ) four.

☐ **1st Speed Reading**

wpm

▶ Comprehension Check

本文を読み、正しい答えを選びなさい。

1. How many people were in the author's group at the coffee shop?
   a. 2   b. 3   c. 4

2. How did the waitress handle the situation?
   a. She tried to fit the author's group into a small booth.
   b. She spoke to the young man in the larger booth.
   c. She got irritated at the author.

3. How does the story conclude?
   a. The author is irritated with the waitress.
   b. The author is irritated with the young man.
   c. The author is irritated with himself.

☐ **2nd Speed Reading**

wpm

▶ Extension Activities

以下の動詞について、活用形を埋めなさい。

現在形	過去形	過去分詞
tell		
move		
begin		
sit		
speak		
understand		
leave		

▶ Write or Speak about Yourself

以下の質問について，答えてみましょう。

Q： **Describe a time when you did or did not "read the room" well.**

A：

Chapter ⑪

接待時のポイント

Entertaining Clients

....

▶ Warm-up Question

....

What are the do's and don'ts of behaviour at a formal event?

example:

be on time

don't order the most expensive thing on the menu

....

▶ Check Your Vocabulary

....

左側の単語にもっとも近い意味をもつ表現を右から選びましょう。

1. venue (n.)   ( )   a. noisy and unpleasant
2. humble (adj.)   ( )   b. to get out of something, usually some form of transport
3. alight (v.)   ( )   c. a place where an event happens
4. raucous (adj.) ( )   d. something difficult that you have to deal with
5. burden (n.)   ( )   e. not proud or not believing that you are important

Ⓝote-taking 🔊 ㉒ 本文を聴きながらノートを取りましょう。（英語でも日本語でも構いません）

1 At a business meal your guests might be pleased if you've chosen dishes from your own country. You can make a good impression if the alcohol used for making a toast is also from your country. You should arrive at the venue before your guests to welcome them. You

5 should $_{50}$ greet them by saying "We've been looking forward to seeing you. Thank you for coming in spite of your busy schedule." When taking an elevator, press the button yourself. When the elevator arrives, allow your guests to enter first. Even in an elevator there is a set order for where $_{100}$ people should be positioned. The left

10 of the back (furthest from the door) is considered to be the place of honor, while the host takes a humble position standing in front of the control panel. When getting off an elevator, your guests should be first to alight. After you get $_{150}$ off you ought to say, "This way please" to show the way. The seating order in a restaurant is

15 basically the same as in a meeting room. It's a good idea to remember the rule: the best seat is the furthest from the entrance. At the start of the meal, $_{200}$ you should greet your guests saying, "Thank you again for taking time out of your busy schedule today." It's better not to talk business straight away. You should start with light

20 enjoyable topics such as small talk, the weather, or hobbies. You must not ask intrusive personal questions. Don't $_{250}$ get raucous or drink too much. Bear in mind that even though you might be relaxed, your behavior should be appropriate to the situation. Sometimes gifts are prepared for when it's time to leave. When handing them over

²⁵ you should say, "This might be a burden, but please take it ₃₀₀ home with you." When they depart, you should see them to the exit （312 words）

🔊 **23**

▶ Dictation

音声を聴いて空欄を埋めなさい。一回目はスロースピード、二回目はナチュラルスピードで録音されています。答え合わせをしたら、音読しましょう。（　/6点）

1. It's better not to talk business （1 　　　　　） （2 　　　　　）.
2. You should start with light （3 　　　　　） topics such as small talk, the （4 　　　　　）, or hobbies.
3. You must not （5 　　　　　） intrusive （6 　　　　　） questions.

☐ **1st Speed Reading**

wpm

▶ Comprehension Check

文章の中で述べられていることに☑マークをいれなさい。

☐ Allow your guests to get out of the elevator before you.
☐ Allow your guests to choose where to sit at the restaurant.
☐ Start by talking about light topics before moving onto business.
☐ Select alcohol from the guests' home country.
☐ Order a taxi or similar transport for your guests to get home.
☐ Do not get to the venue after your guests.

☐ **2nd Speed Reading**

wpm

▶ Extension Activities

以下の動詞について、活用形を埋めなさい。

現在形	過去形	過去分詞
see		
take		
meet		
show		
say		
give		
eat		

▶ Write or Speak about Yourself

以下の質問について，答えてみましょう。

Q： **Describe a time you attended a formal event or dinner.**

A：

Chapter 12

和食

Washoku

....

▶Warm-up Question

....

What are some examples of traditional Japanese dishes?
Which Japanese dishes do you think are well known in foreign countries?

....

▶Check Your Vocabulary

....

左側の単語にもっとも近い意味をもつ表現を右から選びましょう。

1. renowned (adj.) （ 　） a. to include something as part of another thing
2. authentic (adj.) （ 　） b. the feeling that makes you want to eat
3. incorporate (v.) （ 　） c. made in the traditional or original way
4. appetite (n.) 　 （ 　） d. the tired feeling when you have just travelled a long distance on an aircraft
5. jetlag (n.) 　 （ 　） e. famous

Note-taking 🔊 24 本文を聴きながらノートを取りましょう。（英語でも日本語でも構いません）

1   With a reputation for being healthy and tasty, *washoku* (traditional Japanese food) has already become renowned throughout the world. The other day I had the opportunity to have lunch with Michael, a student who had come to Japan for the first time. He is the son of

5   one of my ₅₀ British friends. He told me that sushi is also popular in Britain, and that he wanted to try authentic sushi. So, we dropped in at a traditional sushi shop and ordered a deluxe sushi set. Seeing the sushi, he had this to say. "How wonderful! *Washoku* is like an art ₁₀₀ form; such care is taken over the arrangement of the food, the colors

10   of the toppings and the tableware". Michael began to eat, commenting that it was "delicious," but halfway through stopped using his chopsticks and had the following to say: "Authentic Japanese sushi tastes different from sushi served in ₁₅₀ Britain." In my country there is also delicious sushi available that incorporates

15   meat, fruit, cheese or mayonnaise." It is said that there are now 55,000 Japanese restaurants overseas. Some restaurants serve up *washoku* that Japanese would describe as being substandard; that could hardly be described as *washoku*. In response to ₂₀₀ this situation the Ministry of Agriculture, Forestry and Fisheries is planning to

20   establish a *washoku* certification system for overseas Japanese restaurants, but it seems this will not be easy. Michael gradually slowed his chopsticks, leaving a little bit behind. Not wanting to hurt my feelings, he said, "It was delicious. ₂₅₀ However, I've lost my appetite because of my jetlag." It seemed that the authentic fish-only

25 sushi was not to his taste. Who knows, I thought, before long, people around the world may be eating substandard sushi as authentic sushi and traditional sushi may come to be called "Japanese sushi." On ₃₀₀ returning home, I told this story to my wife. "The ramen that you love originally evolved from a Chinese noodle dish." （323words）

Let's Try

Country Names

国名を探してみよう！（10 カ国）

C	E	M	N	A	N	I	G	E	G
T	O	I	O	G	R	E	E	C	E
M	I	B	C	N	H	R	G	M	T
E	A	B	E	L	G	I	U	M	H
S	O	U	T	H	K	O	R	E	A
U	K	R	A	I	N	E	L	T	I
G	E	R	M	A	N	Y	U	I	L
T	U	R	K	E	Y	L	E	Y	A
U	T	A	B	R	I	T	A	I	N
C	H	I	L	E	M	K	H	I	D

SOUTH KOREA	CHILE
UKRAINE	THAILAND
GREECE	GERMANY
MONGOLIA	TURKEY
BRITAIN	BELGIUM

▶ Dictation

音声を聴いて空欄を埋めなさい。一回目はスロースピード、二回目はナチュラルスピードで録音されています。答え合わせをしたら、音読しましょう。（　　/6点）

1. So, we (1　　　　　　　) in at a (2　　　　　　　) sushi shop and ordered a deluxe sushi set.
2. It is said that there are now (3　　　　　　　) Japanese (4　　　　　　　) overseas.
3. The ramen that you love originally (5　　　　　　　) from a Chinese (6　　　　　　　) dish.

❏ **1st Speed Reading**

wpm

▶ Comprehension Check

本文を読み、当てはまるものを選びなさい。

1. Who is Michael?

   a. the author　　　b. the author's friend's son　　　c. a Japanese language student

2. What was Michael's first reaction to Japanese sushi?

   a. It was really good.　　　　　　　b. It's very similar to sushi in the UK.

   c. It's not as good as sushi in the UK.

3. Why did Michael say he didn't want to continue eating?

   a. The food was making him feel sick.　　　b. He wanted to eat ramen instead.

   c. He was tired after his long flight.

❏ **2nd Speed Reading**

wpm

▶ Extension Activities

寿司の英語

選択肢から選んでみましょう。

日本語	英語
アジ	
イカ	
イクラ	
エビ	
サケ	
タコ	
ホタテ	
イワシ	

octopus	salmon	squid	horse mackerel
scallop	shrimp	sardine	salmon roe

▶ Write or Speak about Yourself

以下の質問について，答えてみましょう。

Q： **Describe your best experience eating an authentic Japanese dish.**

A：

TEA BREAK 和製英語 (Japanese-made English)

和製英語は、「日本で英単語をつなぎ合わせたり変形させるなどして作った語」、つまり外来語をヒントにして作られた日本語のことです。そのため、英語を話す人たちには理解されなかったり、全く異なる解釈をされる場合があります。英語でのコミュニケーションを円滑にするために、和製英語と英語の表現の違いを学び、使い分けるようにしてみましょう。

以下の食べ物に関する和製英語を英語に直してみましょう。

(1) ホットケーキ 　　　　（　　　　　　　　　　　）

(2) ウィンナー 　　　　　（　　　　　　　　　　　）

(3) フライドポテト 　　　（　　　　　　　　　　　）

(4) シュークリーム 　　　（　　　　　　　　　　　）

(5) サイダー 　　　　　　（　　　　　　　　　　　）

(6) コロッケ 　　　　　　（　　　　　　　　　　　）

(7) シーチキン 　　　　　（　　　　　　　　　　　）

(8) ハンバーグ 　　　　　（　　　　　　　　　　　）

(9) アイスティー 　　　　（　　　　　　　　　　　）

(10) ノンアルコール 　　（　　　　　　　　　　　）

Chapter **13**

日本で働く外国人

Foreign Workers in Japan

▶ Warm-up Question

What are the advantages of working in Japan?

▶ Check Your Vocabulary

左側の単語にもっとも近い意味をもつ表現を右から選びましょう。

1. fiscal year (n.) （　）   a. to get something that you want

2. obtain (v.)   （　）   b. the money that you earn, usually from your work

3. immigration (n.) （　）   c. the skills or experience that you need in order to do something

4. income (n.)   （　）   d. the 12 months over which a company calculates its profits or losses

5. qualification (n.) （　）   e. the process of coming to a country in order to live there permanently

Note-taking 🔊 **26** 本文を聴きながらノートを取りましょう。（英語でも日本語でも構いません）

¹ Students graduate in March in Japan, and new employees begin to work in April, when the fiscal year starts. This February the Ministry of Economy, Trade and Industry carried out a survey of foreign students and former foreign students about working environments.

⁵ 83% responded that Japan was an attractive $_{50}$ place to live in, while only 22% replied that it was an attractive place for work. It has been pointed out that foreign students find it hard to adapt to the unconventional customs of Japanese companies, including cleaning the workplace, radio gymnastic exercises, long working hours, and

¹⁰ the difficulty $_{100}$ of taking paid holidays. On the other hand, 70% of university and post-grad graduates wish to work in Japan. However, only about 40% of the students actually obtained a job; this is because 80% of foreign students want to work for a big company, and are not interested in $_{150}$ medium or small sized companies.

¹⁵ However, medium to small sized companies account for 99% of offices and for 70% of total employees. In addition, approximately 60% of these companies aim to employ foreign staff. If foreign students changed their attitude towards medium and small sized companies, it is probable that $_{200}$ the ratio of respondents viewing

²⁰ Japan as an attractive place to work would increase. According to the Ministry of Health, Labour and Welfare, at the end of October 2015, there were about 910,000 foreign workers in Japan, a record high. Approximately 150,000 offices employ foreigners, which is 11.1% higher than $_{250}$ last year. In terms of nationality, China comes top with

25 about 320,000 people (35.5% of total foreign workers), followed by Vietnam, the Philippines, and Brazil. The policy of the Japanese government is to discourage immigration, while being eager to welcome the highly skilled – as long as they meet certain conditions

300 in reference to their profession and income – as well as foreign
30 students who obtain certain qualifications. These "specialized and technical sector" workers number about 170,000, which is 13.6% higher than last year. (332 words)

▶ Dictation

音声を聴いて空欄を埋めなさい。一回目はスロースピード、二回目はナチュラルスピードで録音されています。答え合わせをしたら、音読しましょう。（　　/7点）

It has been pointed out that (1　　　　　　) students find it (2　　　　　　) to adapt to the unconventional customs of Japanese (3　　　　　　), including cleaning the (4　　　　　), radio gymnastic (5　　　　　), long (6　　　　　) hours, and the (7　　　　) of taking paid holidays.

❏ **1st Speed Reading**

wpm

▶ Comprehension Check

本文を読み、あてはまるものを **a, b, c** の中から選びなさい。

1. What reason is NOT given for foreign students struggling to adapt to Japanese companies?

   a. getting little paid time off　　b. having to work out　　c. getting a low salary

2. What percentage of foreign graduates managed to get a job in Japan?

   a. 40%　　b. 70%　　c. 80%

3. Which of the following statements is TRUE?

   a. The number of "specialized and technical sector" workers has increased.

   b. There are more Vietnamese workers in Japan than Chinese workers.

   c. Generally speaking, the Japanese government's policy is to aim for more immigration.

❏ **2nd Speed Reading**

wpm

▶ Extension Activities

事務用品の英語表現

日本語に当たる英語を選択肢から選びなさい。

日本語	英語
のり	
修正液	
物差し	
消しゴム	
画鋲	
蛍光ペン	

thumbtack   whiteout   ruler   eraser highlighter   glue

▶ Write or Speak about Yourself

以下の質問について，答えてみましょう。

Q： **Explain why you do or do not want to work in a foreign country in the future.**

A：

Let's Try

City Names

都市名を探してみよう！（10 都市）

```
G  A  T  H  E  N  S  D  B
P  S  E  O  U  L  N  U  E
A  S  S  N  I  A  L  N  I
R  I  S  G  L  U  E  L  J
I  N  R  K  L  C  E  T  I
S  E  C  O  I  E  D  G  N
T  U  N  N  M  G  N  S  G
A  O  E  G  U  E  N  I  P
H  V  L  O  N  D  O  N  I
```

BEIJING SEOUL
PARIS AUCKLAND
ROME HONG KONG
HONOLULU ATHENS
VENICE LONDON

Chapter 14

日本列島の多様性

Culture and the Japanese Archipelago

....

▶ Warm-up Question

....

What differences are there between the various regions of Japan?

....

▶ Check Your Vocabulary

....

左側の単語にもっとも近い意味をもつ表現を右から選びましょう。

1. vulnerable (adj.) ( ) a. relating to the structure of the surface of the earth

2. tectonic (adj.) ( ) b. easy to hurt or attack physically or emotionally

3. collision (n.) ( ) c. a natural ability that helps you decide what to do without thinking

4. fossil (n.) ( ) d. an accident that happens when two objects hit each other with force

5. instinct (n.) ( ) e. a plant or animal that has been preserved in rock for a very long period

N ote-taking 🔊 **28** 本文を聴きながらノートを取りましょう。（英語でも日本語でも構いません）

1 As a country, Japan has become vulnerable to the effects of climate
change caused by global warming and other factors. About 20
million years ago, a part of the Eurasian continent began to be
gradually cut off by tectonic movement. This became the base of
5 what was later to become $_{50}$ Japan. Then the original shape of the
Japanese archipelago is thought to have been formed about 15
million years ago, after repeated collisions with islands swept away
from the Pacific Plate. All kinds of dinosaurs lived in Japan. Fossil
evidence found all over the country bears this out. The presence $_{100}$ of
10 substances found in the seabed in the Japanese Alps also indicates
uplift caused by tectonic collisions. The north and south of Japan is
divided by a geological fault and the east and west by mountain
ranges. It is therefore common to see clear skies on the Pacific side
of $_{150}$ the country, but snow on the Sea of Japan side, which is
15 separated from the rest of the country by a mountain range. Also,
since the Japanese archipelago stretches a long way from north to
south, while drift ice can be seen at the northern end, the
southernmost end has $_{200}$ coral reefs and warm temperatures. In the
same country, the climate and landscape varies greatly depending on
20 the region. Japan has many beautiful tourist spots such as Mt. Fuji
and Matsushima. On the other hand, Japan has numerous natural
disasters such as earthquakes, tsunamis, volcanic eruptions, and
typhoons. It's $_{250}$ said that this natural environment has had a great
influence on the development of the character of the Japanese

25 people. This is why the Shinto religion, based on the belief that Gods reside everywhere in nature, took root here. An instinct to find a way to coexist with nature and $_{300}$ help each other out gave rise to Japan's unique culture. Furthermore, the presence of four distinct seasons together with other natural blessings, such as hot springs, have also

30 created a unique culture in the region. (334 words)

▶ Dictation

音声を聴いて空欄を埋めなさい。一回目はスロースピード、二回目はナチュラルスピードで録音されています。答え合わせをしたら、音読しましょう。（　　/6点）

1. In the same country, the (1 　　　　　　) and (2 　　　　　　) varies greatly depending on the (3 　　　　　).

2. On the other hand, Japan has (4 　　　　　) natural disasters such as (5 　　　　　), tsunamis, volcanic eruptions, and (6 　　　　　).

☐ **1st Speed Reading**

wpm

▶ Comprehension Check

文章をよく読み、正しい（ **T** ）、間違い（ **F** ）、この文章からは読み取れない（ **?** ）のいずれか、あてはまるものを記入しなさい。

1. A long time ago, Japan was part of the Eurasian continent. （　　）

2. There are more dinosaur fossils in Japan than in any other country. （　　）

3. The Japanese character is said to have been shaped by the natural environment. （　　）

☐ **2nd Speed Reading**

wpm

▶ Extension Activities

地理に関する重要単語

選択肢から選んでみましょう。

日本語	英語
経度	
緯度	
インド洋	
大西洋	
太平洋	
北極	
南極	
赤道	

equator	Pacific Ocean	south pole	latitude
longitude	Atlantic Ocean	north pole	Indian Ocean

▶ Write or Speak about Yourself

以下の質問について，答えてみましょう。

Q： **Describe a time you traveled in Japan. What regional differences did you notice?**

A：

公用語　(official language(s))

公用語とは、「ある国や地域でおおやけの場での使用が定められている言語」のことです。日本の公用語は、法令などで規定されていないものの、事実上、日本語が公用語となっています。公用語は、1つの言語とは限りません。多民族国家では、複数の言語が公用語として認められています。たとえば、シンガポールでは、英語、中国語、マレー語、タミル語の4つ言語が公用語として認められていますが、これら4つの言語が使用される割合は、その言語を使用する人口によって異なります。したがって、公用語は、「国が公式使用のために認めた言語」であり、国民が実際に話せる言語とは限らないという現実があります。

以下の各国の公用語を選択肢から選んで、記入してみましょう。（2回以上使う選択肢もあります）

(1) ベルギー　　　　　　　（　　　　　　　）（　　　　　　　）（　　　　　　　）

(2) フィンランド　　　　　（　　　　　　　）（　　　　　　　）

(3) ケニア　　　　　　　　（　　　　　　　）（　　　　　　　）

(4) エジプト　　　　　　　（　　　　　　　）

(5) パキスタン　　　　　　（　　　　　　　）（　　　　　　　）

(6) フィリピン　　　　　　（　　　　　　　）（　　　　　　　）

(7) ミャンマー　　　　　　（　　　　　　　）

(8) カナダ　　　　　　　　（　　　　　　　）（　　　　　　　）

(9) ブラジル　　　　　　　（　　　　　　　）

(10) メキシコ　　　　　　　（　　　　　　　）

ビルマ語	ウルドゥー語	スワヒリ語	スウェーデン語
スペイン語	ポルトガル語	フランス語	英語
オランダ語	タガログ語	アラビア語	フィンランド語
ドイツ語			

Chapter **15**

日本型宅配サービス

Japanese Home Delivery Services

▶ Warm-up Question

Do you think Japan home delivery services are good? What are the good points about them?

▶ Check Your Vocabulary

左側の単語にもっとも近い意味をもつ表現を右から選びましょう。

1. resident（n.）　　（　　）　　a. to make someone admire or respect you
2. designate（v.）　（　　）　　b. someone who lives in a particular place
3. impress（v.）　　（　　）　　c. to choose something for a particular purpose
4. subscribe（v.）　（　　）　　d. a period of time between two activities or events
5. interval（n.）　　（　　）　　e. to pay money so that you regularly receive a service or product

Note-taking 🔊 **30** 本文を聴きながらノートを取りましょう。（英語でも日本語でも構いません）

1 One of the services non-Japanese residents in Japan admire is express home delivery. With Japanese express home delivery, items are not just picked up at your home, but it's also possible to pay by cash on delivery and designate an arrival time. In addition, if the
5 expected package does not $_{50}$ arrive on schedule, you will be able to find out where it is by phoning the delivery company. The other day I had an opportunity to talk with Marco, a young man who came from South America to Japan, and our conversation turned to this topic. "My country, too, has $_{100}$ home delivery service, but I'm
10 impressed by the Japanese service," he said. And he continued, "Recently, a package was delivered when I was out of the house, and an absent contact notice was put in my postbox." I said, "Surely they do this in all countries?" Then Marco said, "Yes $_{150}$, but there isn't a service that redelivers at a time to suit me when I call the telephone
15 number written down." I was surprised that he is impressed by a service which is regarded by Japanese as something to be expected. Sometime later, I got a message from Marco on $_{200}$ my answerphone saying "Call me back please." Thinking that something had happened to Marco, I called him at once. He had this to say. "I
20 subscribe to a Japanese newspaper for my Japanese studies, but recently went for a one-week-long trip. When I told a friend about this he said $_{250}$, 'The newspapers will pile up in your postbox and it'll be easy to tell you're away; you'll be a target for thieves.' Taking his advice, I instructed the newspaper delivery company to stop

25 delivery during my trip." Then, he continued to explain excitedly. "On the day I returned from my ₃₀₀ trip, a bag containing the newspapers from that interval was hanging on the entrance doorknob. On the bag was written, 'Welcome home. We kept your newspapers. Thank you for reading.'" I told Marco, "I understand

30 you were touched by Japanese out of home services, but you should know ₃₅₀ that when the person you want to speak to is out, in Japan it is good manners to call again." (370 words)

▶ Dictation

音声を聴いて空欄を埋めなさい。一回目はスロースピード、二回目はナチュラルスピードで録音されています。答え合わせをしたら、音読しましょう。（　　/6点）

When I told a （1　　　　　　　　） about this, he said, 'The （2　　　　　　） will
（3　　　　　　　） up in your （4　　　　　　　） and it'll be easy to tell you're
（5　　　　　　）; you'll be a target for （6　　　　　　　）.'

❏ **1st Speed Reading**

wpm

▶ Comprehension Check

Marco について、あてはまるものに☑マークをつけなさい。

☐ He lives in South America.

☐ He thinks the Japanese home delivery service is very good.

☐ He thinks the home delivery service in his home country is as good as Japan's.

☐ He reads a Japanese newspaper to help him learn the language.

☐ He asked for his newspapers not to be delivered when he took a trip.

❏ **2nd Speed Reading**

wpm

▶ Extension Activities

日本の慣用句

慣用句になるように、空欄に当てはまる語を選択肢から選んでみましょう。

日本語	英語
百聞は一見に如かず	Seeing is （　　　　　　　　）.
七転び八起き	Life is full of ups and （　　　　　　　　）.
転ばぬ先の杖	Better safe than （　　　　　　　　）.
飴と鞭	The carrot and （　　　　　　　　）.
本末転倒	Put the cart before the （　　　　　　　　）.
二足の草鞋を履く	Wear two （　　　　　　　　）.

downs	stick	hats	horse	sorry	believing

▶ Write or Speak about Yourself

以下の質問について，答えてみましょう。

Q： Describe another service in Japan that you think is very good.

A：

SOUND
DOWNLOAD

テキストの音声は、弊社 HP　https://www.eihosha.co.jp/
の「テキスト音声ダウンロード」のバナーからダウンロードできます。
また、下記 QR コードを読み込み、音声ファイルをダウンロードするか、
ストリーミングページにジャンプして音声を聴くことができます。

Japan Explained:
Japanese Culture through Authentic Texts
日本文化の魅力と多様性

2024 年 1 月 15 日　初　版

著　者 ⓒ 津　田　晶　子
ⓒ 金　志　佳　代　子
ⓒ Ｃｈｒｉｓ　Ｖａｌｖｏｎａ

発 行 者　佐　々　木　　　元

発 行 所　株式会社　英　　宝　　社
〒 101-0032 東京都千代田区岩本町 2-7-7
電話 03-5833-5870　FAX03-5833-5872
https://www.eihosha.co.jp/

ISBN 978-4-269-17027-8 C1082
印刷・製本：日本ハイコム株式会社